FUERTEV

Stunning beaches and a landscape that will amaze you

For permission requests, contact the Author at :-

stepheninfo9@gmail.com

ISBN : 9798842538287

Stephen Cartledge
296/ M12 Phan Prao
Ampheo Si Chiang Mai
Nong Khai. Thailand.

+66 0909591958

Welcome to paradise, where the magic begins and memories last a life time.

INTRODUCTION

Fuerteventura with it's Kilometres of heavenly white or golden sand beaches with turquoise waters, this is the perfect snapshot for anyone who loves feeling the sun, the sea breeze and taking revitalising swims in calm, transparent waters. The list is endless; there are so many reasons to visit Fuerteventura, it would be difficult to mention all of them. You don't have to go far to make this dream image a reality any day of the year. It's right here, in Fuerteventura, to enjoy intensely and without hurrying, and it's only a few hours away from the main European cities.

Fuerteventura is the second largest Canary Island out of the eight main islands are (from largest to smallest in area)

CANARY ISLANDS

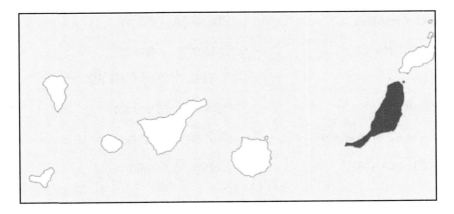

- Tenerife

- Fuerteventura,

- Gran Canaria

- Lanzarote

- La Palma

- La Gomera

- El Hierro

- La Graciosa.

It is located 84 km to the east from Gran Canaria and 11 km to the south from Lanzarote. It is the closest one of the Canary Islands to Africa. At one point the distance to the Moroccan coast is only 95 km.

GEOGRAPHY

Location	**Atlantic Ocean**
Coordinates	**28'20'N 14'1'W**
Archipelago	**Canary Islands**
Area	**1.659.74 km 640.83 sq mi**
Coastline	**304 km 188.9 mi**
Highest elevation	**807 m 2648 ft**
Highest point	**Pico de Zarza**

The island is divided into six municipalities.

- Antigua

- Betancuria

- La Oliva

- Pájara

- Puerto del Rosario

- Tuineje

Puerto del Rosario is the Islands capital city with a population of, 40,753 as of the year ending 2019.

The landscape on Fuerteventura is quite different from that on the other islands. The first thing you will probably notice is that the mountains are not that high and not that broken. The highest point on Fuerteventura, Pico de la Zarza or also known as Pico de Jandia, is only 807 metres above sea level. Most of the "mountains" including Pico de Jandia are located on the small Jandia Peninsula in the south-western end of Fuerteventura (the part of the island closest to Gran Canaria).
Jandia Peninsula is connected with the rest of Fuerteventura by the 5 km wide Pared Isthmus (Istmo de la Pared), which is the narrowest point of the island. The larger northern part of Fuerteventura is rather flat.
This is because Fuerteventura (together with the neighboring Lanzarote) is the oldest of the Canary Islands. It probably first appeared above the sea level more than 20 million

years ago. The last volcanic activity on Fuerteventura occurred about 4,000 years ago.

To visitors this island is best known for its long beaches covered either with white sand or black volcanic shingle. Due to the island's proximity to Africa and its surface the climate on Fuerteventura is very warm and very arid. Average annual precipitation is only 147 mm. On the other hand, sandstorms (known as calima) are common. They bring sand from the Sahara and can rapidly increase temperature for a while.

The climate on Fuerteventura is mild, but you must be aware that it is mostly windy, throughout the year. The island is hence referred to as the island of eternal spring.

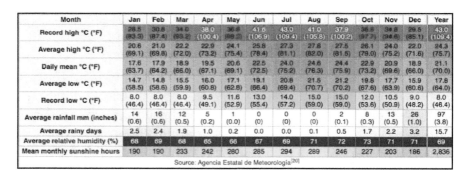

Month	Jan	Feb	Mar	Apr	May	Jun	Jul	Aug	Sep	Oct	Nov	Dec	Year
Record high °C (°F)	28.5 (83.3)	30.8 (87.4)	34.0 (93.2)	38.0 (100.4)	36.8 (98.2)	41.6 (106.9)	43.0 (109.4)	41.0 (105.8)	37.9 (100.2)	36.8 (97.7)	34.8 (94.6)	29.5 (85.1)	43.0 (109.4)
Average high °C (°F)	20.6 (69.1)	21.0 (69.8)	22.2 (72.0)	22.9 (73.2)	24.1 (75.4)	25.8 (78.4)	27.3 (81.1)	27.8 (82.0)	27.5 (81.5)	26.1 (79.0)	24.0 (75.2)	22.0 (71.6)	24.3 (75.7)
Daily mean °C (°F)	17.6 (63.7)	17.9 (64.2)	18.9 (66.0)	19.5 (67.1)	20.6 (69.1)	22.5 (72.5)	24.0 (75.2)	24.6 (76.3)	24.4 (75.9)	22.9 (73.2)	20.9 (69.6)	18.9 (66.0)	21.1 (70.0)
Average low °C (°F)	14.7 (58.5)	14.8 (58.6)	15.5 (59.9)	16.0 (60.8)	17.1 (62.8)	19.1 (66.4)	20.8 (69.4)	21.5 (70.7)	21.2 (70.2)	19.8 (67.6)	17.7 (63.9)	15.9 (60.6)	17.8 (64.0)
Record low °C (°F)	8.0 (46.4)	8.0 (46.4)	8.0 (46.4)	9.5 (49.1)	11.6 (52.9)	13.0 (55.4)	14.0 (57.2)	15.0 (59.0)	15.0 (59.0)	12.0 (53.6)	10.5 (50.9)	9.0 (48.2)	8.0 (46.4)
Average rainfall mm (inches)	14 (0.6)	16 (0.6)	12 (0.5)	5 (0.2)	1 (0.0)	0 (0)	0 (0)	0 (0)	2 (0.1)	8 (0.3)	13 (0.5)	26 (1.0)	97 (3.8)
Average rainy days	2.5	2.4	1.9	1.0	0.2	0.0	0.0	0.1	0.5	1.7	2.2	3.2	15.7
Average relative humidity (%)	68	69	68	65	66	67	69	71	72	73	71	71	69
Mean monthly sunshine hours	190	190	233	242	280	285	294	289	246	227	203	186	2,836

Source: Agencia Estatal de Meteorología[20]

The cuisine is fairly basic due to the customs and climate conditions. They share this simplicity with the other Canary islands, and similarly to them, they use a large quantity of fish. They also use whatever they can grow in the near-barren land. This includes papas arrugadas, a dish of wrinkled potatoes usually served with mojo, which is a hot pepper sauce or with puchero Canario, a meat stew. This is one of my Favourite dishes.

Seafood is prepared in many ways traditionally, such as pejines (salted fish), jareas, or sancocho (a type of stew) made from fish, generally the grouper, corvina or sama, boiled after salting, and served with mojo, potatoes, or gofio (a type of grain). People are also very keen on the mussels and limpets collected on the island's coasts.

They also use meat such as beef and pork to make different dishes or simply to for braising, but their main meat is goat, both from the kids and from the older animals. They eat the goat roasted or stewed. Goats are not only useful for their meat – the Fuerteventurans also use the milk to make the cheese majorero, which has won many prizes. The majorero is mostly made of goats milk, and occasionally it is up to 15% ewes milk. It is cured in pimento oil or gofio meal. Majorero and palmero cheese are the only two Canarian cheeses with protected denomination of origin.

So what is so attractive about Fuerteventura? You are currently planning your next trip and you wonder what is all this hype around Fuerteventura? let me take you on a journey of the Island from my personal experience of my years living in Fuerteventura.

CHAPTER 1 BEACHES

1.1 It's incredible beaches

The beaches of Fuerteventura are simply breathtaking, magnificent and whatever adjectives you want to give it. There is something for everyone and you will rarely come across a beach crowded with tourists. Almost 150 kilometres of picture-perfect beaches and only one problem: picking which one to visit! An issue that can easily be solved by going to a new one every day. I will take you to some large beaches surrounded by endless dunes; the little ones can have a safe swim in the crystal-clear lagoons that form between sandbanks and natural reefs; you might feel a bit more adventurous and we can go as far as the wild solitary beaches, which have been the sets of major film productions, or take a boat trip to a little islet off the coast for some unforgettable moments.

1.2 The Sand Dunes of Corralejo

The Parque Natural de las Dunas de Corralejo is one of the most-visited natural areas in Fuerteventura and boasts the largest sand dunes of the Canary Islands. With miles of near-white sand beaches, clear turquoise waters, huge dunes and a contrasting red and black volcanic landscape, it is real natural gem of the Canary Islands.
The Natural Park covers around 24 km², including the beaches, the large shifting sand dunes and the volcanic landscape to the south. Known locally as Grandes Playas

(big beaches), the 10 Km stretch of coastline is actually made up of a number of smaller beaches. These pale sandy beaches have few rocks and clear turquoise waters. Contrary to many guides and newspaper articles, the sand here has not "blown over from the Sahara", but is in fact composed of the shells of marine creatures.

Although this area may seem rather barren, there are a number of species present. The Houbara Bustard is the flag-bearer of the Natural Park and is the largest native bird in the Canary Islands.
You may also see little egrets, spoonbills, kentish plovers, lizards as well as beetles and other invertebrates. Very few plants can survive such harsh conditions, two exceptions, having adapted to the shifting sand dunes are Androcymbium gramineum psammophilum and the Sea Grape (Tetraena fontanesii). Importantly, the park, along with the nearby island of Lobos are designated as a Special Protection Area for Birds (ZEPA – Zona de especial protección para las aves).

The area was designated as a Natural Park in 1982 together with the small island of Los Lobos, located just off the coast of Corralejo. Unfortunately two large hotels were built before the area was declared a protected space. These Hotels are rather a blot on such a stunning landscape, however on the plus side, if you stay in either of the hotels, the dunes and turquoise waters really are on your doorstep.

The Grandes Playas are great for water sports. An area known as Flag Beach is a favourite with surfers in the area. The El Medano area is often visited by wind and kite surfers. With 10 Km of coastline, there is plenty of space on the beaches for everyone, including those wanting to catch some rays. However, as great as the area is for water sports, it is not that great for swimming, as there are strong currents and rip tides along with a small ratio of lifeguards to beach-goers.For those wanting a more tranquil day at the beach, head for the zuccos. These semi-circular stone shelters provide some respite from the wind and offer a little privacy too – they are often occupied by nudists, especially towards the southern end of the dunes.

Dotted along the beaches are a number of Chiringuitos (beach bars) along with toilet and shower facilities. Though a few areas offer sun-loungers and umbrellas for hire, there is very little cover in the Natural Park, so ensure that you bring plenty of sun cream and water with you. For those wanting the best views, bring suitable footwear and water and head up Montaña Roja (Red Mountain). This 314 m volcano in the south of the park offers stunning 360 degree views and is a great spot for photography on a clear day.

You can walk to the dunes from Corralejo – it takes around 1½ to 2 hours from the centre of town. You can also cycle, catch a bus, grab a taxi and some hotels even offer a shuttle service. The Natural Park is a must-see for visitors to Fuerteventura, but even peak season, if you hire a car, you will usually find a parking spot and definitely a place on the beach. Since 1987, every November, kite flyers from all over the world have come to compete and join in what is now a weekend long Kite Festival held in the Corralejo Natural Park. If you are in the area at the beginning of November, then I would highly recommend heading into the park to take a look.

CORRALEJO SAND DUNES

FV 1 ROAD TO CORRALEJO

2. El Cotillo

In my early days of living in Fuerteventura, I was fortunate enough to rent a 2 bedroomed villa only a few kilometres way from El Cotillo, so we visited the lagoons quite often with our two small children.

El Cotillo beach sits on Fuerteventura's west coast and consists of white, clean sand and rocky outcroppings. Sheltered from breaking waves, this fabulous beach is picturesque and stunning. Visitors enjoy impressive ocean views and miles of sandy beaches to explore. You will not find rows of sun-beds and umbrellas at El Cotillo, as you would on many of Fuerteventura's other beaches. Instead, beach goers enjoy wonderful, natural beaches with fine sand and clear water.

The beach is clothing optional and nude sunbathers are prevalent, so bear this in mind when planning your visit. You might even consider joining the fun!

La Concha is one of Fuerteventura's best-known beaches for its beauty, quality and tranquility. The beach's close proximity to the town allows you enjoy a break with incredible sea views and amazing sunsets, where the sky changes from ochre to violet in a matter of minutes. La Concha beach enjoys gentle waves thanks to its natural horseshoe-shaped reef. When the wind picks up the 'corralitos', small circular walls made from volcanic rock built by residents, are the perfect refuge, and at low tide the children can play safely in the small rock pools that form. There is parking very close to the beach and a lifeguard service as well as a restaurant nearby.

In addition to the beach, El Cotillo is known for its tranquil lagoons which are protected by a natural reef from the

Atlantic's thunderous surf. Visitors can snorkel, swim or paddle in these calm, shallow areas. As with many other of Fuerteventura's beautiful beaches, windsurfing and kiteboarding are popular activities. If you're spending time on Fuerteventura, you could do far worse than enjoying a day at El Cotillo!

A visit to La concha beach is a must whilst you are in Cotillo. These lagoons at Cotillo make this an ideal beach area for smaller children.

LA CONCHA BEACH

EL COTILLO LAGOONS

3 Caleta de Fuste

This is the place I spent the most of the time whilst living in Fuerteventura.

Also known as "El Castillo" or more colloquially as "Shank's Shark", Caleta de Fuste is one of Fuerteventura's most popular beaches thanks to its proximity to the airport as well as the city of Puerto del Rosario — the island's capital.

Over 800 meters long, Caleta de Fuste beach is popular with families and offers an exhaustive array of activities for all age groups. Caleta de Fuste provides safety and security to its guests with a lifeguard patrolling its sun-strewn sands and separate areas for swimming and water sports. Caleta de Fuste Beaches – Central & La Guirra.

Yes there are two beach areas in Caleta de Fuste – the central beach in the resort centre, and the La Guirra beach to the south in front of the Sheraton, Carlota and Sara Hotels.

3.1 Central Beach

The central beach in Caleta de Fuste is man-made and gently slopes into the sea. The sea is never rough as the beach is protected by the harbour.

The sea is safe for children to paddle or swim in the shallows, but you have to take care with the prevailing north-easterly winds which can easily blow lilos, inflatable dinghies, swim rings and balls out to sea very quickly.

There are also goalposts and volleyball nets for beach games, and there is plenty of space for organised games. During the summer season, beach games and bouncy castles are usually held at the back of the beach on one day of the week. There is a children's playground and beach gym at the back of the beach.

There are wooden boardwalks on the beach to allow easier access for wheelchairs to reach the sea, wooden solariums and a bathing chair for people with reduced mobility.

3.2 La Guirra Beach

In front of the Sheraton, Carlota and Sara Hotels, and the Atlantico Center is La Guirra beach. This is a man-made lagoon style beach with golden sand. The sea for swimming there is ideal as the water is deep enough, yet is protected from waves by rock barriers out at sea.

CENTRAL BEACH

LA GUIRRA BEACH

4. **Playa de Gran Tarajal**

Gran Tarajal is Fuerteventura's third-largest city and is located on the southeastern shore of the island. Playa de Gran Tarajal is the city beach, located near the harbour and fronted by a beautiful bay. At approximately one kilometer long, the beach is set against the beautiful backdrop of the city's pastel-washed houses and is a perfect spot for relaxing. A lively promenade lines the beach and offers visitors their choice of cafes, restaurants and bars.

Gran Tarajal is an enticing destination for swimmers and divers as well as kite boarders and windsurfers, luring them with clear, shimmering water and golden sand. There are also sporting facilities available on the beach for active visitors including a football field and a volleyball net. An extensive children's playground is also present.

A lively promenade lines the beach and offers visitors their choice of cafes, restaurants and bars.
Playa de Gran Tarajal reflects the laid-back city from which it derives its name. This sleepy town has not yet been the subject of heavy tourism, and most of the beach's visitors are local residents. If you're searching for a quiet getaway, and a low-key alternative to some of Fuerteventura's busier beaches, you'd be hard pressed to find a better place to unwind than Playa de Gran Tarajal.

GRAN TARAJAL

GRAN TARAJAL

23

5. Sotavento Beach

Sotavento Beach is located in Costa Calma in Feurteventura's southeastern shore. Spanish for "calm coast", it is an exceptionally pristine beach spearheaded with jagged outcrops of volcanic rock. No surfers will be found here as the beach fronts some of the calmest waters on the island. Only the gentlest waves lap the shore, making Sotavento a truly amazing choice for swimmers.

With it's miles of untouched beachfront unfurl southwards from the resort of Costa Calma – that's Playa de Sotavento. It's one of the most popular on the island because it caters to all sorts of visitors. It's also stunningly beautiful, with a series of shifting sandbanks that break the ocean up into small, glittering lagoons.

The locals separate Satavento into several sections. La Barca, in the north, has conditions for kitesurfing. Walkers, birdwatchers, and photographers are often most taken by Risco del Paso and its unique sand spits. Down south in Malnombre, you'll find wind guards built out of the volcanic rock and sunbathers for whom beach fashion isn't a concern,

Occasional strong winds make this a favorite spot for windsurfers and kite boarders, and visitors may be tempted to join in the fun as courses and equipment are available for rent at the nearby windsurfing school.

There's plenty of room along the beach for kids to play and for couples to enjoy a romantic stroll at the water's edge. Just offshore, jet-skis and boats rule the water and are also available for hire to visitors.

Playa Barca - Sotavento. The Fuerteventura World Cup takes place every year over the second half of summer and consists of several competitions, namely PWA Windsurf Freestyle Grand Slam, PWA Windsurf Slalom Grand Slam, and GKA Kite surf Strapless Freestyle Grand Slam.

This High Wind Spot in Fuerteventura allows you to watch world stars in windsurfing and kiteboarding, closer than anywhere else. Along with the breathtaking World Championship contests, you'll be able to savour delicious specialities and discover the local cuisine. A Colorful support programme with live music and various entertainments for the whole family perfectly completes the festival atmosphere. Check out the legendary World Cup Parties. These vibes will keep you awake until dawn.

SOTAVENTO BEACH

WALK WAY SOTAVENTO BEACH

6. Playa de Cofete

Windswept beach combing sessions under muscular mountains.
The Jandía Peninsula, in the southernmost part of Fuerteventura, is home to one of the largest and most majestic treasures of this Canary Island: the Playa de Cofete beach. Hidden in the windward part of the peninsula, this incredible beach—measuring more than 12 kilometers long—remains something of a secret, shielded by the mountain range of the Jandía Natural Park. The peninsula's mountain range drops abruptly on the same side as the Cofete beach. This, combined with its difficult access, makes it a practically virgin beach.

The Playa de Cofete beach is unquestionably one of Fuerteventura's most special beaches, with each visit guaranteed to be an unforgettable experience.
Playa de Cofete is a wild and blustery length of beachfront that hides beyond the mountains of the Jandia Natural Park. Facing the brunt of the Atlantic Ocean on the extreme south-western edge of Fuerteventura, it's a far cry from your picture-perfect, come-laze-on-me white sand.

Instead, it's one for the hikers and photographers. Swirls of ocean mist and sea spray often dance across the dunes and the mountains. There's a stark contrast between the coffee-coloured peaks and the blue of the water. Rip currents are too strong for swimming, but you could scale Pico de la Zarza. It's the highest point on Fuerteventura and offers one of the best views of Cofete.

PLAYA COFETE

PLAYA COFETE

CHAPTER 2 LANDSCAPE

The spectacular landscapes of Fuerteventura leave breathless even the most impassive traveller. The astonishment that the spectators feel contemplating the nature and landscapes of this island does not cease to amaze and surprise them.

The island of Fuerteventura was declared a World Biosphere Reserve by Unesco. In its Parks and Natural Monuments, you will find incredible landscapes to see and photograph that, being protected spaces, conserve their genuine nature. Mountains, volcanoes, beaches, all landscapes of Fuerteventura possess incredible beauty that will not leave you indifferent.

Within the most outstanding landscapes of the northern area, in the municipality of La Oliva, you will find the Natural Park of Corralejo with its incredible dunes, areas with volcanoes such as the Monument of the Malpaís de La Arena or the Calderón Hondo, the Cueva del Llano , the Tostón Tower, the Barranco de Tinojay with its rock engravings, the Barranco de los Encantados or Enamorados, the Mirador de Vallebrón, the Caima Mountain. In Cotillo beaches you will find white sand beaches and excellent waves for windsurfing.

To the northwest, the Magic Mountain of Tindaya was considered sacred by the ancient aborigines of the island. It represents a site of high archaeological interest for the rock engravings that have been found there, also it tells about magical rites that generated fantastic legends that have been handed down for generations. There is a natural cave known as the Bailadero de las Brujas.

Tindaya Mountain is in the north of Fuerteventura and is one of the many mountains scattered throughout this part of the island. However, Tindaya is much more than just a mountain. It is a mountain blessed with mystery and history; a mountain considered sacred by the indigenous people of the island; a mountain where many stone engravings from the pre-Castilian era have been found.

Only these engravings remain from the times when the Mahos – indigenous people from Fuerteventura – performed rituals on Tindaya. The engravings are called "podomorfos", because they are shaped like feet, and their purpose has not been widely agreed on by historians.

2.1 Tindaya: Sacred Mountain

In the pre-colonial era, Fuerteventura was inhabited by a Maghrebi ethnic group from North Africa. And for some Maghrebi ethnic groups, uncommon geographical features, including mountains, had a sacred character, as they were attributed to a manifestation of the power of nature. They believed that some natural monuments were inhabited by gods and should be worshipped.

In Fuerteventura, the indigenous peoples worshipped many different manifestations of nature, but the most important was Tindaya Mountain, which they believed was a kind of personification of the gods. The role of the engravings is still debated in the research community. While some believe that they served as symbols of partnerships and marriages; others believe that they are drawn where the Mahos would impart justice, and the engravings symbolize the prisoners feet.

Others think that the engravings are born from different religious rituals and indigenous beliefs, such as offerings to the Gods in exchange for water. Given that many engravings point towards Mount Teide, some researchers interpret that the Mahos believed that the Devil lived on Mount Teide, due to the strong volcanic explosions that they saw from Fuerteventura.

And so the legend of Tindaya was born – a mountain 401 meters tall and full of mystery. Only its walls and engravings remain as eyewitnesses of what really happened here: sacrifices, religious rituals, alliances, justice…

Towards the southwest of the island, is the Castle of Lara in the Natural Park of Betancuria, an ideal place to go with children. Don't miss the outstanding landscapes offered by touring the Ajuy caves and enjoying a sunset on the beach of this area.

To the south, the Jandía Natural Park occupies a large part of the Jandía Peninsula. It is one of the highest peaks of the island, La Zarza. From there you can see the arch of the Cofete and the ravines of Vinamar and the one of the Butihondo Valley.

In the peninsula of Jandía is also one of the wildest beaches on the island, the Playa de Cofete, ideal for the more adventurous visitors as to access it you have to take a roughly paved road. Sotavento Beach, an extensive shore with fine white sand and crystal clear waters, with some dunes near the sea that recreate a desert.

Just 2 km offshore from Corralejo is the small island of Isla de Lobos. Literally translated as the island of Wolves, the term comes from the Spanish word for Mediterranean monk seals (sea wolves), which once inhabited the small island.

Although Isla de Lobos has not had a permanent resident since 1982, tourists visit via day-trips from Corralejo Harbour to enjoy the islands tranquillity, crystal-clear turquoise waters, walk the trails and observe nature.

In the Isla de Lobos you will find fantastical landscapes to photograph and create unique memories to bring home. The terrestrial landscapes are wonderful, but so are the submarine sceneries thanks to the crystalline waters of the sea and its marine life. The island is inhabited by a great variety of species of birds that live there all year round or pass during some periods in their migrations to other regions.

The island measures just 4.5 Km², with a coastline of just over 14 km. There is only one village on the island – the tiny El Puertito (little port), which is little more than a few basic fishing huts. These are now mostly used by local fishermen's families for recreational purposes during the summer months.

You can walk around the entire island in a few hours, though you should add an extra hour or so if you plan to walk up the steep slope of Montaña la Caldera. There are no roads on the island and you must stick to the clearly defined walking paths it is prohibited to walk elsewhere and there are wardens patrolling.

The island was designated a natural park in 1982 along with the Parque Natural de Corralejo. It is also zoned as a Special Protection Area for Birds (ZEPA – Zona de especial protección para las aves) and is an important nesting site for seabirds such Cory's Shearwater, Bulwer's Petrel, Storm Petrel and others. The small amount of plant life that survives here has is drought-tolerant and able to cope with high salinity, such as the endemic siempreviva bushes that blanket areas in pinks and purples.

Interestingly, Isla de Lobos contains the archaeological site of a recently-discovered Roman settlement. The ancient settlement made purple-blue dye from sea snails – a very smelly business, and probably the reason why this activity took place on an offshore island. It is believed that 10-12,000 snails were required to make just 1 gram of purple-blue dye, which partly explains why this colour was only worn by the highest of aristocracy. The site is usually covered to protect it from wind and sand, unless excavation work is in progress.

One of the most photographed locations is the horseshoe-shaped cove, Playa de la Concha (sometimes called Playa de la Caleta). Its crystal-clear waters, light golden sand and protected waters make it a great spot for snorkeling and swimming. At the far end of the beach is a sculpture in memory of the seals that once inhabited the island. To get to Playa de la Concha (Shell Beach) head left from the jetty.

In the North-East of the island, you will find the Faro de Lobos (Lobos Lighthouse) located at Punta Martiño. The lighthouse, built in 1865, is one of the oldest in the Archipelago and originally ran on olive oil. It was automated in the 1960s and the building remains locked, though there is an information board outside for visitors.

Although it is off-limits during the breeding season (ask), many people climb the Caldera de la Montaña – the highest point on the island at 127 m. This semi-circular-shaped hill is the remains of a volcano that has been partly eroded by the sea, and affords stunning views of Lobos, Lanzarote and Fuerteventura from its summit. This walk is best tackled early in the day, especially in the heat of summer, though you can always head to Playa de la Concha to cool off afterwards.

There is one very small family-run restaurant in El Puertito, though you need to reserve/book food before noon, if you plan to eat there.

Do bear in mind that there is very little shade on the island other than at the visitor centre (which also has public toilet facilities). Therefore visitors to the island should ensure they bring plenty of water and sun-cream (along with food, if you don't plan to eat at the restaurant.

It takes around 15 minutes by boat from Corralejo Harbour and there are a number of vessels operating on this route.

TINDAYA MOUNTAIN

CHAPTER 3 WHERE TO STAY

There's so many beautiful places to stay in fuerteventura, all offing something different. I will list below what I think to be the 5 most popular places to stay which I have visited.

1. CORRALEJO (best for first-timers)

2. COSTA CALMA (best for sports)

3. EL COTILLO (best for couples)

4. MORRO JABLE (best for a local atmosphere)

5. CALETA DE FUSTE (best for families)

3.1. Corralejo

The road from the airport to Corralejo has some of the best views! Just picture a long highway with sand on both sides and the bluest sea. It literally looks like a painting made with the best colours ever! With its laid-back atmosphere and lively harbour, Corralejo is your traditional Spanish vacation spot. Corralejo is definitely the best place to stay in Fuerteventura if you're visiting the island for the first time because there's something to do here for any type of person. Located in the north part of the coast, this resort town is an oasis of sugary sand dunes and blue crystal water! Honestly, You'll find some of the best beaches here, some of which are especially suited to families traveling with kids.
If that sounds a little too calm for you, there are tons of beaches ready for anyone who's into surfing too! You have to try out those Spanish waves, they are amazing! Let's not forget the most beautiful and famous beach in Corralejo, the

6 miles (10 km) Playa Grande, where the white sand dunes meet the sea and create a magical picture. You can explore the town and harbour area at night, that's when the restaurants and bars get ready to show their tourists an amazing time! Speaking of the harbor, Corralejo is also a great spot to stay if you want to do some island hopping as you can take a ferry to Lanzarote in 30 minutes

3.2 Things to do in Corralejo

- Spend a fun day at the Acua Water Park
- Enjoy a family day out at the Corralejo Viejo beach
- Explore the nightlife of Corralejo in the harbour
- Have a drink at the many friendly Karaoke & Disco Bars
- Go surfing at Playa del Medio
- Visit the Corralejo Natural Park
- Learn a new language and a new water sport with the Spanish & Surf school

MAIN STREET CORRALEJO

CORRALEJO TOWARDS HARBOUR

3.2.1 Costa Calma

Located on the south of the island, just a 1 hour drive from the airport, Costa Calma is a beautiful area that is perfect for surfers and anyone who is coming to Fuerteventura to try all the possible activities and water sports. You'll find some of the best beaches here and the winds and small waves favour those who want to try windsurfing or kitesurfing. You can also try snorkeling, jet skiing, surfing, or kayaking! The beach is not the only big attraction here, if you stay on this part of the island you'll be able to experience the unique Sunday Market in town. I loved attending these cute gatherings while I lived here. You get to taste the most delicious fruits and vegetables and go shopping for little souvenirs that will remind you of your holiday.

Costa Calma doesn't really have a town center, however, you'll find a road along the coast surrounded by nature dotted with beach resorts, small shopping centers, bars and restaurants. Make sure to book your accommodation in advance, especially during the summer as the best hotels here sell out fast!

3.2.2 Things to do in Costa Calma

- Enjoy sunbathing on the Costa Calma Beach
- Try windsurfing on Playa de la Barca
- Take the kids to the quiet Pájara Beach in Costa Calma
- Go surfing on Sotavento Beach
- Explore the Afrikanischer Markt (Costa Calma African Market) and go shopping for souvenirs

COSTA CALMA BEACH FRONT

COSTA CALMA SHOPPING CENTER

3.3 El Cotillo

Located on the north west side of the island and filled with whitewashed houses and white sand, El Cotillo is Fuerteventura's best spot for romantic walks on the beach and tranquil sunsets near the cliffs. This remote town used to be a fishing village and although it became popular among tourists, not everyone hurries to come here. That means that couples can enjoy some peace and quiet! And have you seen the pictures? I feel like this spot should definitely appear in one of those romantic movies!
What's more, during those hot summer days the ocean breeze here cools you down perfectly. This will only help you to enjoy the local vibe of the town even more.
If you catch the view of the tiny white houses during the golden hour you'll feel like you were transported to a whole different world. Here everyone is super friendly, calm and just wants to live by the sea all their life! For an unforgettable experience, go to the Los Lagos beach which has the most amazing lava lagoons and turquoise waters!

3.3.1 Things to do in El Cotillo

- Eat seafood in the best restaurants in town
- Watch the sunset with your loved one at El Cotillo Beach
- Visit the Torre del Tostón fortress
- Spend a fun day near the lagoons at Playa Los Charcos III
- Go sunbathing and swimming in the turquoise waters at Los Lagos beach

EL COTILLO LIGHTHOUSE

EL COTILLO CLIFFTOP

4.Morro Jable

Located right on the southern end of the coast around a 75-minute drive from the airport lies Morro Jable, tucked away between the cliffs. This lovely fishing village has managed to keep its authentic local atmosphere even though it's a popular holiday spot on the island, especially among German tourists. The little whitewashed houses and white sandy beach look like they've been taken straight out of a postcard! The picturesque seafront promenade leads the path towards the old town and the harbour where you'll find many restaurants and bars that, as you might've guessed, have the best seafood dishes possible. It is a fishing village after all! This town has amazing resorts, popular among families with small children and this part of the island also has a cool local market which takes place every Thursday. If you come all the way here you have to visit one of the most famous beaches on the peninsula, Playa de Cofete. Playa de Cofete is surrounded by the highest cliffs on one side and the most magical turquoise water on the other and is located not too far along the coast from Morro Jable on the Jandia Peninsula. It's reachable by public transport or you can rent a car and get there in under an hour on mostly dirt roads.

4.1 Things to do in Morro Jable

- Go sunbathing and swimming on Playa del Matorral
- Take a trip to visit Casa Winter to learn some interesting history
- Take a night walk on the Playa De Jandia beach in Morro Jable

- Explore the old town part of Fuerteventura in Morro Jable
- Play a round at Jandia golf course
- Take a trip to visit the amazing beach at Playa de Cofete and the Jandia Peninsula in the nearby Jandía Natural Park

MORRO JABLE SHOPPING STREET

MORRO JABLE BEACH WALKWAY

45

5.Caleta de Fuste

Located on the east coast, this resort town is close to the airport and filled with bars, restaurants, and great hotels perfect for families who are traveling with small children. This part of the island has a laid back atmosphere and is very calm, the seaside promenade offers amazing views of the whole town and it's a lovely place where you can take long walks at sunset.

The family-friendly beach in Caleta de Fuste resort town is quite big and the winds aren't as strong here, which means it's a safe spot for kids and you'll find all the facilities you need like sun beds and umbrellas. If you also want to explore other parts of Caleta de Fuste, there are plenty of golf courses in this area.

There's also a cinema if you want to catch a family movie, a shopping center and for an authentic local experience, you can head to the weekly market to get some nice island souvenirs.

5.1 Things to do in Caleta de Fuste

• Have some family fun on the Playa del Castillo

• Take some time off from the beach and play a match at the Fuerteventura Golf Club

• Learn new things about the island's history at the Castillo de San Buenaventura

• Take the kids to the Oceanarium Explorer to play in the waterpark or swim with seals

CALETA SHOPS

CALETA MARINA

CHAPTER 4 ONE FOR THE GOLFERS

Fuerteventura is a great year-round destination for golfers. Sunshine hours in abundance, less rainfall than the more westerly Canary Islands of Gran Canaria and Tenerife and the challenging trade winds (love it or hate it, it certainly makes the game interesting). And when you're not out on the course, there are more beaches than on any other Canary Island, plenty of water sports, cycling and hiking on offer, as well as all of the benefits of being in a tourist destination that is open 12 months of the year.

In Caleta de Fuste you will find Fuerteventura's first and only PGA championship rated golf course. Opened at the end of April 2002. it earned it's title when it staged the 2004 Spanish Canaries Open to much acclaim.

Covering 1,500,000 sq. meters it has some superb views to the Atlantic ocean with lakes and palm trees. The fairways, tees and rough are all planted with two varieties of Bermuda with agrostis seaside at the fringes and at the grens, agrostis Penn A4.

Although there are 67 bunkers, none are too deep. It lies a few minutes from the sea and golden sandy beach at Caleta de Fuste. Designed by Juan Catarimeau it has been thoughtfully designed with the prevailing north, north westerly wind in mind. Less than 10 Km from the airport is the tourist resort of Caleta de Fuste, which has two 18 hole courses. This area is favoured by golfers, given the short distance between the two courses and their proximity to the airport. If you get an early-enough flight over, you can be on the course by the early afternoon.

4.1 Fuerteventura golf club

This course was designed by Juan Catarineu in 2002 with a focus on one thing the island has plenty of, wind! One bragging right of the club is that The Spanish Open was played here in 2004. Special rates are available for guests of the Elba hotels, of which there are three in Caleta, one being the adults-only 5 star Elba Palace Golf & Vital Hotel.

Facilities Include:

- 18 Holes
- Driving Range
- Putting Green
- Chipping Green
- Shop
- Buggies/Clubs & trolley rental
- Golf lessons/courses
- Restaurant at the 5* Elba Palace Golf & Vital Hotel within the grounds.

4.2 Salinas de Antigua golf club

The course was designed by double world champion Manuel Pinero and is located just next door to the more established Fuerteventura Golf Club.

Facilities Include:

- 18 Holes

- Driving Range

- Putting Green
- Chipping Green
- Shop
- Buggies/Clubs & trolley rental
- Restaurant
- Golf lessons/courses

FUETEVENTURA GOLF CLUB

SALINAS DE ANTIGUA GOLF

4.3 Jandia golf club

The course was designed by the very experienced Ron Kirby and alternates long and short holes within the stunning Barranco de Vinamar. The course was unfortunately closed for more than 5 years but re-opened in September 2014 after significant investment and course upgrades.
The course offers a number of play and stay options, in both the on-site hotel and in the nearby Barcelo (many reviews state that the Barcelo is far better).The local Robinson Jandia hotel (the first to be built in Jandia back in the 1960's) also hosts tournaments at the course.

Facilities Include:
- 18 Holes
- Driving Range
- Putting Green
- Chipping Green
- Shop
- Buggies/Clubs & trolley rental
- Cafe/ Bar
- Golf lessons/courses

JANDIA GOLF

CHAPTER 5 OFF THE BEATEN TRACK

Inland Fuerteventura retains its peaceful charm. There are rolling plains dotted with ancient windmills, the spectacular barren mountains of the Parque Natural de Betancuria, small oases of palm trees and sleepy towns and villages such as Betancuria itself - the island's original 15th-century capital - and Pajara, with its impressive 17th-century church. Everywhere you'll find the locals making and selling their traditional crafts of basketwork and ceramics. Don't miss out, get out there as see for yourself.

You will be surprised how many hidden gems there are out in Fuerteventura.

5.1 Aguas Verdes

Aguas Verdes is a 6 km long stretch of natural lagoons on the West coast. A wonder of nature, unspoiled and wild. The terrain is beautiful and rugged. They are a bit hard to get to, so i would recommend of of the buggy trips that are available round many resorts, or you could hire your own 4x4. Whilst you visit,be mindful of tide times and weather. It's also very dangerous for swimming, so just come to watch the waves, meditate with the ocean and be in awe with nature.

5.2 Montaña del Cardón

The Montaña del Cardón Natural Monument is located south of the town of Pájara, and is made up of the remains of an ancient volcanic building. Montaña de Cardón is a mountainous massif with an interesting differential erosion that has been influencing the place for several million years, giving rise to an imposing landscape in the shape of a knife-back that houses on its slopes the jorjado, which is a endemic plant species on the island.

The highlight of this mountain is its visual impact due to the fact that it is located in a low-lying area, in addition to attracting attention with its reddish colors. From its summit you can get a spectacular view of the Cofete area and the "volcanic pythons" (remains of the conduits of the volcano through which the eruptive material came out) are striking. On the eastern slope of the mountain is the "Ermita del Tanquito", easily accessible and where a pilgrimage is held every year from the town of El Cardón.

5.3 Verdeaurora Bio Farm

Verdeaurora Bio Farm is the place that gives the opportunity to feel nature at its best, to connect with ourselves and with a pure and pollution-free environment, where tradition and sustainability coexist in perfect harmony. In this little piece of Fuerteventura we take care of what matters most to us, our planet, and we share it with those we love most.

The day to day in this typical Majorera farm is characterized by the certified organic production of Aloe vera and olive trees, for the creation of pure and natural care products. In addition, those staying at the Bio Farm, and also visitors to the island, live a unique experience: tour every corner of the crops by day and, at nightfall, fall head over heels in love with a star-studded sky. Verdeaurora Bio Farm offers a farm/food+sky observation experience once per week with a professional astronomer.

5.4 fishing village

Ajuy's most outstanding attraction is its natural caves, that were declared a Natural Monument in 1987. Located in the Rural Park of Betancuria, they are protected for their high natural value and their impressive beauty. These caves, which are over a hundred centuries old, represent the most ancient formations in the Canary Islands and they are one of the 150 places with major geological importance in the world. The path to the caves starts from the beach of Ajuy and it is a 500 meter walk where visitors can understand the geology of the island.

Besides its caves, the fishing village of Ajuy attracts visitors for its charm and position: far away from hotel complexes, it offers a relaxing visit for you to pause and rest. Ajuy is oriented towards the sea, close to a ravine and a nice black sand beach, Playa de los Muertos, that leads to a truly wild coast. It is one of the few black sand beaches in Fuerteventura and it reminds us of the volcanic origins of the Canary Islands.

AGUAS VERDES

MONTANA DEL CARDON

VERDEAURORA BIO FARM

AJUY FISHING VILLAGE

CHAPTER 6 SPECIAL EVENTS

6.1 Fuerteventura Kite Festival

Three days full of fun, pleasure, colour, and wind.
Every year in November, La Playa del Burro, a beach
situated in the dunes of Corralejo becomes a main stage for
the International Kite Festival. Since 1987 the beauty of this
event has been drawing more and more people from around
the globe. The variety of kites' shapes and colours is truly
amazing. People that have visited this event once usually
end up returning again and again. There's even a club
named "The Fuerteventura Kite Family" which includes
people who were present at the first festival and since that
time have come every year. This event lasts for three days.
Everything starts on Friday when everyone is invited to let
his or her kite fly. This day is also called a "free fly." On
Saturday people show their craftsmanship and skills of
controlling their kites. There is also a night display on
Saturday. Sunday offers the biggest fun. More than a
hundred kites are given out to children. Little Teddy bears
even parachute and drop sweets. There is also a battle
between two kites till one falls from the sky. And, of course,
lots of prizes are given to the participants.

KITE FESTIVAL

6.2 Windsurfing & Kitesurfing World Cup.

If you are a windsurfing and kitesurfing fan, you can't miss the greatest world cup ever on an island called "The Great Adventure"
Fuerteventura (Great Adventure), the second largest Canary Island in Spain, hosts one of the most exciting sporting events every year: Windsurfing & Kiteboarding World Cup also known as Fuerteventura Grand Slam. Recognized as one of the world's greatest competitions, the World Cup has taken place here for over 30 years and the show is truly fantastic. The island's landscapes and water provide an amazing natural arena for both men's and women's freestyle and racing events. The festival can appear dangerous and exciting at the same time!
The Fuerteventura World Cup takes place every year over the second half of summer and consists of several competitions, namely PWA Windsurf Freestyle Grand Slam, PWA Windsurf Slalom Grand Slam, and GKA Kite surf Strapless Freestyle Grand Slam. This High Wind Spot in Fuerteventura allows you to watch world stars in windsurfing and kiteboarding, closer than anywhere else. Along with the breathtaking World Championship contests, you'll be able to savour delicious specialities and discover the local cuisine. A colourful support programme with live music and various entertainments for the whole family perfectly completes the festival atmosphere. Check out the legendary World Cup Parties. These vibes will keep you awake until dawn.

SURFING CHAMPIONSHIP

KITEBOARDING CHAMPIONSHIPS

6.3 Canarian Day

This is a major Fiesta in the Canarias. Like many Spanish Fiestas it tends to last for more than just a day. The celebrations start in May and continue for 4 days.
Canarian Day 2022 is the 39th yearly event celebrating the first meeting of the Autonomous Canarian Government on May 30th 1983. The Canaries gained Independence from Spain in August 1982. If you are in Corralejo at the time of the event, you might have notice that a stage is being built by the Hoplaco Roundabout on the Main Street This will be one of many focal points during the celebrations. Be sure to have a good walk around, to find everything this fiesta has to offer.
There will be stalls selling local produce throughout the 4 day celebrations giving you the chance to sample traditional Canarian produce. Usually on the third day, they all join in the Baile de Magos celebrations. Singing, dancing and drinking to Traditional Canarian bands while watching the traditional dance troupes.
The final part of the celebrations is a big street party where tables and chairs are laid out for the locals, who bring their own picnics with them. This is a fantastic experience and though some may think it's only for the locals, tourists are made to feel welcome. They can take their chance to make fools of themselves by joining in and copying some of the traditional dances.
All in all, the music is outstanding, the songs often unintelligible (except to the Majoreros) and the traditional dancing is great to watch, but not recommended to attempt.
A great few days of celebrations, with a friendly party

atmosphere, have a few drinks, get into the party mood. Relax and absorb the ambience of Canarian Day.

CANARIAN DAY

6.4 El Cotillo Fiesta and Music Festival

The El Cotillo fiesta always takes place at the end of August and lasts roughly 10 days. During this time the village is transformed from a quiet laid-back place into a very busy, noisy one. Don't expect much sleep at this time!

Many expats who live in the village leave and go on holiday elsewhere to get away from it as sleep can be hard to get. The music (if some of it can be described as that) goes on until 4-5am or even later sometimes.

Whether you are likely to enjoy the fiesta or not if you are staying in El Cotillo when it is on might depend on your age. Much of the entertainment is aimed at teenagers and is basically very loud music which goes on until it gets light (and beyond). Teenagers from all over the island, and even further afield, come to El Cotillo for this.

There are quieter, more traditional, aspects to the fiesta. These include the fishermen's procession from the old harbour which takes place on a Sunday afternoon.

The statue of the Virgin of the Safe Voyage is carried from the little church in the village and then loaded on to one of the fishermen's boats – an honour it seems. It is then taken for a little cruise out to sea and back for 15 minutes. All the other boats follow the boat with the statue aboard.One evening there is a concert of traditional Canarian music, usually on the quayside. This is one of the few musical events during the fiesta which isn't too loud!

On the last Saturday night there is a firework display in the old harbour which always attracts large crowds. This takes place after the the Virgin of the Safe Voyage is carried back from the little church to the church in El Roque where it spends the rest of the year.

Music Festival

This takes place one weekend in early July. A large stage is built in the car park of Shell Beach (Playa de la Concha). The music takes place on a Friday and Saturday night from sunset to perhaps 4am. Although this is located quite a way outside the village, because the music is so loud, it can still be heard everywhere. My first rented house was in La lajares which was only 5 minutes away from La Concha beach. I'll never forget that first carnival we attended, wow what an experience. Bands from all over Spain, the Canary Islands and even South America are invited to appear in the concert. Some of them are very good, some are ok and others are just noise.

The council operates free buses from the village to the concert site and also extra buses normally run from both Corralejo and Puerto del Rosario into the small hours.

EL COTILLO FESTIVAL

6.5 Three King's Parade

In most of the large towns on the island there are 3 King's parades on the 5th January (usually in the evening) . The Kings ride camels and after the parade they collect the children's wish lists. On the night of 5th Jan/6th Jan the Kings deliver presents to children (and some adults) while they are sleeping. It is a more important festival than Christmas here.

Festivities begin on January 5th on the eve of Día de los Reyes Magos (Three Kings Day, January 6th), referred to as 'Spain's Second Christmas'. According to tradition, the three kings Melchior, Caspar, and Balthazar, from Europe, Arabia, and Africa followed a star for 12 days until they came to Bethlehem. Bringing with them gifts of Gold, Frankincense and Myhrr.

In the evening children across Fuerteventura line up their shoes by the door, along with food to feed the camels. When morning arrives, children discover presents and sweets, and if they have misbehaved, lumps of coal. Locals typically share a Roscón de Reyes (King's Bread) to mark the event, a sweet dough in the shape of a crown, and embellished with candied fruits, sugar, and sweets.

3 KINGS PARADE

CHAPTER 7 MORE FESTIVALS

Festivals, fairs and religious pilgrimages in Fuerteventura

The people of Fuerteventura know how to have fun, and there is always a good excuse to go out into the streets, or the fields in the case of religious pilgrimages. Join the party and enjoy because you will most likely come across a celebration during your stay.

7.1 La Candelaria in La Oliva

On the 2nd of February, the village of La Oliva spares no expense to celebrate the festival in honour of Our Lady of La Candelaria, the patron saint of the Canary Islands. Although the best-known image of Our Lady of La Candelaria is from the nineteenth century and located in the Tenerife town of the same name, residents of Fuerteventura's La Oliva are proud to have a statue of this Black Madonna that dates back to the late fifteenth century. In fact, it is one of the oldest Christian icons in the Canary Islands. La Oliva celebrates its patron saint in style with numerous events featuring bands of street musicians, music festivals, open-air dances and religious acts that include a procession through the town carrying the beautifully adorned Virgin.

7.2 Antigua Artisan Fair

The village of Antigua is famous for its handicrafts, among other things. In fact, it has a handicrafts centre housed in a traditional mill that is definitely worth a visit.

During the first half of May, the municipality hosts the Insular Artisan Fair, which is held in an 8,500-metre venue and welcomes more than 20,000 visitors. It showcases woodworking, costume jewellery and leather goods with an original, indigenous touch that are available for purchase.

7.3 Virgen de Regla festival in Pájara

The festivities to honour Our Lady of Regla take place in Pájara on the 2nd of June. Starting the previous week, residents fervently devote themselves to the festival, which has countless activities for all ages. The main event is the religious pilgrimage that begins at the interesting seventeenth-century hermitage where the image is located. It continues through the municipality, and residents wear traditional garb as they are accompanied by carriages.
Day of Saint Bonaventure, a festivity in Betancuria
The festival of Saint Bonaventure, patron saint of Betancuria, takes place on the 14th of July. As the oldest festivity on the island, it became official by Diego de Herrera in 1456, when resistance by local aborigines was declared to be under control of Castilian colonists. he procession in honour of the patron saint is particularly interesting because it features rondalla serenade groups who add an attractive musical note to the event. Virgen del Carmen festival in Morro Jable Located on the southern end of Fuerteventura, Jandía Bay hosts the traditional boat procession that accompanies Morro Jable's Virgen del Carmen, the patron saint of the sea. After the procession, pilgrims and visitors eat by the shore at one of the many fish grills along the sand or at one of the nearby inns or beach bars.

7.4 Virgen de la Peña religious pilgrimage

The third Saturday of September marks the festivities honouring the Virgen de la Peña, the patron saint of Fuerteventura. The sanctuary is located on the outskirts of Vega de Río Palmas, in the Peña ravine (to which it owes its name). According to legend, this is where the image miraculously appeared before San Diego.
The Madonna with Child is a gorgeous French Gothic alabaster sculpture that is believed to have reached the island with the first French expedition to the island in 1402. On the big day, visitors and pilgrims from all over the island visit the sanctuary of Virgen de la Peña to pay tribute.
Tran Tran International Clown Festival in Gran Tarajal
The Gran Tarajal Tran Tran International Clown Festival, featuring more than 100 circus artists from all over the world, takes place in September. A treat for children and adults alike!
Over the course of a weekend, 60 performances will bring a smile to everyone's face. Firmly established within the island's events calendar for cultural activities, Tran Tran welcomes more than 20,000 visitors every year.

7.5 Virgen del Rosario festival in La Oliva and Puerto del Rosario

The first Sunday of October, the La Oliva and Puerto del Rosario municipalities celebrate the festivity for Our Lady of the Rosary. Puerto del Rosario is adorned with all types of decorations and there is an extensive activities program to celebrate the day of its patron saint.

7.6 Battle of Tamasite festival on 13 October

Recently declared of National Tourist Interest, the re-enactment of the Battle of Tamasite by Tuineje residents takes place on Gran Tarajal Beach every 13 October. On this date in 1740, a ship carrying English pirates invaded the coast of Gran Tarajal. Locals bravely went into battle and were able to fend off their attackers using sticks and stones. This historic feat is remembered with a faithful and elaborate re-enactment that will amaze those who come to witness it.

Main roads in Fuerteventura

Key to Symbols

🛍 Shopping
△ Good Beach
✝ Church or Cathedral
🔲 Site of Historic Interest
☑ Golf Course
⌐ Water Sports
i Tourist Information

Corralejo   Los Lobos

El Cotillo

La Oliva
La Matilla

Casillas del Angel

Puerto del Rosario

Betancuria   Playa Blanca

Puerto de la Pena   Antigua

Caleta de Fuste

Pajara   Puerto De la torres

Tuineje   Pozo Negro

Las Playitas

Tarajalejo Gran Tarajal

Punta De los Molinillos

Costa Calma

Playa de Sotavento de Jandia

Morro Jable   Jandia

Approx scale: 29km

WHY FUERTEVENTURA

This is a question so many people ask before booking a holiday.
So let me give you the low-down on why Fuerteventura is one of Britain's most loved holiday destinations.

With its year-round toasty climate, travelling to Fuerteventura will feel as though you have reached the tropics.
Fuerteventura caters for a wide range of needs. Whether you're a couple looking for good food and a relaxing beach or a family looking for great activities, you're sure to find your perfect holiday in Fuerteventura.

Enjoy some family time at Acua Waterpark or take in the breath-taking views of the golden sand dunes. Relax on the endless stretches of white sand beaches or dance the night away at the discos and bars.
Here are six top reasons why you should go to Fuerteventura.

• No time difference

• Just a four-hour flight time

- Fuerteventura is a fairly small island so despite having different resorts, all towns are easily accessible

- Over 125 miles of golden and volcanic sandy beaches

- Over 300 days of sunshine and temperatures rarely outside of 18 and 27 degrees Celsius.
- Safe and calm environment.

Happy holidays, this is where the magic begins.

8. Lets talk about the weather.

One of the most frequent questions asked on the
Fuerteventura Forums is-
What's the weather like, is it too cold to swim in the sea?
So before we rush off to book our holidays, lets look a little at
the climate, month by month.

When is the best time to visit Fuerteventura?
When rain does occur it is usually between late October and
March and it brings a touch of green to the North-West part
of the Island and the mountainous areas around Betancuria.
However, it is still scarce enough around the main resorts on
the East coast to ensure that the landscape remains desert-
like all year round. Many visitors claim that the best time to
visit the Island is September and the first half of October; the
weather is still summer-like at this time, the trade winds are
at their lightest and the sea is at its warmest.

Climate Overview
The climate of the Island is classified as a hot desert climate
according to the Koppen-Geiger classification and is
influenced by many factors: the North-East Trade Winds,
subtropial-latitude, proximity to Lanzarote, proximity to
Africa, lack of altitude and the relatively cold Canary Current.
According to Unesco, Fuerteventura is home to the largest
area of desert and semi-desert in Europe.
Unlike the Western Canary Islands (and like its nearest
neighbour, Lanzarote), Fuerteventura does not have high
mountains. This means that the moisture-laden air just
passes over the Island without depositing rain. The only
exception to this is at the peaks of Jandia in the very South
of the Island, which just about makes it into this zone.

Lanzarote, although also a low-lying island, also provides a mild rain shadow effect as it lies to the North-East of Fuerteventura (the direction of the prevailing wind). For this reason, Fuerteventura does not experience the pronounced difference in cloudiness between the North and South that is experienced in most of the Canary Islands.

Sea Temperatures

The cold Canary current means that water temperatures are slightly cooler than you might expect at this latitude – although at 22 or 23 degrees Celsius in late summer, they are still very pleasant.

Calima

Sometimes (usually during the summer) the wind changes to a more Easterly or South-Easterly direction, bringing the dust-haze or 'Calima' along with searing temperatures from the Sahara Desert.

Micro-climates

There can be quite a bit of variation in weather conditions from place to place according to time of year. Costa Calma can become very windy at certain times of the year (there is a reason why the Windsurf and Kitesurf Championships are held at nearby Playa Sotavento), while nearby Morro Jable is sheltered by the Island's highest mountain range. Sea conditions also vary considerably around the Island: Surf might be up in El Cotillo, while it is flat calm in Jandia. Corralejo is often cloudy in the morning, but this tends to 'burn-off' as the day progresses. The driest, sunniest and warmest part of the island is Morro Jable – where it is often 2 or 3 degrees warmer than in the North.

And while Caleta de Fuste might not offer the most spectacular beaches on Fuerteventura, the sheltered lagoon can offer water temperatures that are several degrees higher than in the open sea.

January Weather in Fuerteventura

Daytime High Temperatures
As you might expect, and by nearly every measure, January is the coldest month of the year in Fuerteventura. Average daily highs are just under 21°C – although it will often feel hotter on south-facing sun terraces that are sheltered from the wind (usually the case in Fuerteventura). Some days will, of course, be hotter, and there are usually some 23°C or 24°C days during January.

Night-time Temperatures
At night, temperatures in most places along the coast typically drop to about 14°C or 15°C, perhaps a degree or so warmer in sheltered locations in the south such as Morro Jable. Inland, temperatures drop a few degrees more, especially in the mountains. Some years are hotter or colder than others, and the lowest nighttime temperature ever recorded at the airport is 9°C. The usual advice to visitors is that shorts and t-shirts are fine during the day, but you might need a cardigan or light jacket at night.

Rain in January
January is, on average, the second rainiest month of the year (after December). However, remember that Fuerteventura is a desert island, so the second rainiest month only gets 2-3 days of rain (over 1mm) and a total of just 12.9mm. From experience, I would say that the rainy

days tend to come on consecutive days as a weather system slowly passes through the islands.

Cloud Cover
There are some clouds on most days, with, on average, just 2 overcast days during the month. The north of the island is cloudier than the south, something worth bearing in mind at this time of year if you are looking to maximise sunshine hours during your holiday.

Wind
January is not usually the windiest month of the year on the island, though there can be some blustery days if there is stormy weather.

Sea Temperature
The temperature of the sea is about 19°C in January, so okay for short dip in a shallow bay on a sunny windless day, but you will probably require a light wetsuit if you plan to spend any time in the water surfing, snorkelling or diving.

Calima
Episodes of dust being blown over from the Sahara are more common at this time of year. Although searing temperatures are unlikely (the Western Sahara is cool at this time of year), the thick dust is quite unhealthy, and the government may advise people to avoid outdoor exercise.

In January, the sun rises just before 8am and sets at about 18:20.

February Weather in Fuerteventura

Daytime Highs

February is one of the colder months in Fuerteventura, with average daily highs of about 21°C – though there are usually some 24 or 25 degree days (Celsius). It will often feel warmer on sheltered sun terraces, and temperatures are usually 1 or 2 degrees warmer in the far south than in the north of the island.

Nighttime Low Temperatures

At night, temperatures drop to around 15°C along the coast in the northern half of the island, but are about a degree and a half warmer in Morro Jable (16-17°C). Inland, temperatures drop a few degrees more, and it can get chilly at night in the mountains. The lowest temperature ever recorded at the Airport was 7.6°C in February 2018 – about 4 degrees colder than the average coldest night of the year. In short, temperatures are usually warm enough for shorts and T-shirts during the day, but you will likely need a cardigan or jacket at night.

A Chance of Rain

There is a chance of rain in February, with an average of 3.7 days of rain above 0.1mm (2.4 days over 1mm). The average rainfall for the entire month at the airport is 15.9mm, however this figure is heavily skewed by the occasional torrential downpour, and there is often no rain at all during the month of February.

Cloud Cover

The east coast gets an average of 2-3 overcast days during the month – a slightly skewed statistic caused by some particularly cloudy years. Corralejo tends to be cloudy in the morning, with that cloud evaporating, or 'burning off' by midday. In the south, it tends to be sunnier, especially in Morro Jable.

Cold Sea Temperatures
The sea is at its coldest in February in the Canary Islands at around 18°C. That's around the same temperature as the coast of England in July, so it may be warm enough for some hardy people, but not for everyone! If you plan to do any water-based activities, such as surfing, snorkelling or diving, you will definitely need a wetsuit.

Wind
February is not a particularly windy month in Fuerteventura, with an average wind speed of about 20kmph at the Airport (other parts of the island are less or more windy). It can be gusty though, particularly if there is some mixed weather passing through.

Anecdotal Observations
The numbers quoted above are from the Spanish Meteorological Agency (Aemet), however they do not tell the whole story. From experience, February can be a very mixed month weather-wise, during some years, there can be beach weather all month (the sea is always cold in February though), other years can be cloudy. Between January and March, there are usually one or two weeks of cloudy and rainy weather. Unfortunately, these spells tend to last for about a week, so some visitors are just unlucky with the timing of their week-long break.

March Weather in Fuerteventura

Daytime Highs

Daytime high temperatures typically reach just over 22°C in March – though it is not uncommon to get some days with highs of as much as 28°C – perhaps even 30°C in the south. Thermometers around sun-terraces often read quite a bit more than the official figures at this time of year as the sun gets stronger. However, you can be unlucky with the weather in March, as there is the possibility of a bad week of rainy or unsettled weather.

Temperature at Night
At night, temperatures around the coast drop to 15 or 16°C – perhaps a degree warmer in Morro Jable, and perhaps a degree or two colder in the centre of the island. Some nights may be slightly warmer (or colder), though you will still likely need more than a T-shirt if you plan to sit outside at night.

Rain in March
On average, Fuerteventura gets about 3 days of rain in March – a number that seems fairly constant based on personal observations in recent years. That is to say, that Fuerteventura nearly always gets at least 2 days of rain in March. The median total precipitation for the month is just 8.3mm – so even when it rains, it is very little compared to anywhere in Northern Europe. Having said that, a torrential downpour is not unheard of in March either.

Cloud Cover
There are normally some clouds in the sky during March – especially in the north of the island. If it is overcast in Corralejo in the morning, then this may well 'burn off' or evaporate by midday. The south is generally sunnier, so a drive to the south of the island may be worth a punt if it is

remaining overcast in the north. On average the whole island will be overcast for about 2 days during the month.

Wind
With an average wind speed of 21kmph, March is not one of the windier months on the island. However there can be some very windy days during the month.

Sea Temperature
In March, the sea remains cold around Fuerteventura at about 18-19°C. This might be okay for a quick dip if you are hardy, but if you plan any surfing, wind surfing, snorkelling or diving, you will probably want a wetsuit.

Conclusions
The weather can be somewhat unpredictable in Fuerteventura in March: you could be basking in 30°C sunshine on the beach, or it could be rainy and cool (20°C). It will almost certainly be cool at night (15 – 18°C). In short, you will likely enjoy some warm days at the beach, but you may need some slightly warmer clothes at night such as a cardigan or fleece.

April Weather in Fuerteventura

Daytime Highs
Daily high temperatures typically reach 22 – 24°C in April, with some days reaching 26 – 28°C. Sheltered spots in the sunshine will feel quite a bit warmer, and the sun can be very strong – so make sure you use plenty of sunscreen. The breeze can lure people into a false sense of security, leading to some nasty sunburn.

Nighttime Temperatures

Temperatures at night typically drop to around 16°C along the coast in April, though there can be a marked difference between the north and south of the island, with nightly lows 1-2°C warmer in Morro Jable than elsewhere. Locations exposed to the trade winds in the south, such as Costa Calma, can also be quite cool at night.

April Showers?

In Spain, there is a saying: "En abril, aguas mil" inferring to an abundance of rain, however, this does not apply to Fuerteventura. The island receives, on average, just two days of rain during April, and by 'rain' we mean days that receive more than 0.1mm. The average total rainfall during April is 5.3mm – a long term average brought up by the years that received torrential downpours. A more meaningful total is 2.1mm (median), and many years receive no rain at all. As with most months, the south of the island is drier than the north.

Cloud Cover

There are usually some clouds visible in the sky in April: this is most pronounced in the northern half of the island, and out over the sea. In Corralejo, it is sometimes overcast in the morning, but usually hot and sunny by the afternoon. The south of the island is mostly sunny all day, with a few clouds in the sky.

Windy?

As the summer trade winds start to take hold, the north-easterlies become more constant and April gets an average wind speed of about 23kmph. This helps to keep the temperature down, but can also lead to a false sense of security with the strong sun. If you find it too windy on a given beach, it is worth exploring others nearby: for example, Playa del Matorral in Jandia is often very windy, while the neighbouring Playa de la Cebada in Morro Jable is usually sheltered. The beaches in Corralejo town are also generally less windy than the Corralejo Dunes.

Sea Temperature
The sea surface temperature is typically around 19°C in April, and many people are surprised to learn that the sea is actually warmer in December than it is in April. 19°C water will feel pretty cold to most, but is probably okay for a quick dip on a hot afternoon. Otherwise, if you plan to spend a long time in the water, you will probably want a summer wetsuit.

As the summer trade winds start to take hold, the north-easterlies become more constant and April gets an average wind speed of about 23kmph. This helps to keep the temperature down, but can also lead to a false sense of security with the strong sun. If you find it too windy on a given beach, it is worth exploring others nearby: for example, Playa del Matorral in Jandia is often very windy, while the neighbouring Playa de la Cebada in Morro Jable is usually sheltered. The beaches in Corralejo town are also generally less windy than the Corralejo Dunes.

May Weather in May

Daytime High Temperatures
Temperatures typically reach 24°C in the afternoons in May – though this has been rising in recent years and you will likely encounter several 24 – 28°C days. There isn't much variation in temperature around the coast of the island at this

time of year, though temperatures in the interior may be higher.

Nighttime Lows
Temperatures drop at night to about 17°C on average, though this can vary quite a bit with some years averaging 16°C and others as high as 19°C. Morro Jable in the south tends to be at the higher end, with places like El Cotillo in the north at the cooler side. In summary, some nights may be tropical at this time of year, while there is still a chance of needing a light jacket or cardigan during cooler evenings.

Rain in May
Rain is pretty unlikely in May in Fuerteventura. The average total rainfall on the island during May is just 5.4mm, and the median closer to zero, meaning that, in most years, there is no rain at all.

Cloudy?
The northern part of the island is often cloudy during the first half of the day at this time of year, with plenty of strong sunshine in the afternoon. The south of the island is usually sunny all day.

Wind
The trade winds (Alisios) are more constant at this time of year, meaning that there is a more continuous breeze. With this in mind, it is often a good idea to seek out those beaches that are protected from the prevailing North-easterly winds. If you are sunbathing in a breezy location, remember that the sun is very strong – many people don't realise that they are getting badly burned because of the cooling breeze.

Sea Temperature
The sea remains fairly cold in May at just over 19°C. You might be surprised to learn that the sea is warmer in December in the Canaries than it is in May. Consequently, the sea might be warm enough for a quick refreshing dip at this time of year, but you'll likely need a wetsuit if you plan to spend a long time in the water.

June Weather in Fuerteventura

Daily High Temperatures
In June, temperatures reach 25 or 26°C on most days, with some days over 30°C. The sun is very strong at this time of year: remember that Fuerteventura is less than 100km off the coast of the Sahara Desert!
Nightly Lows
The average minimum temperature in June is 19.1°C, with some years averaging over 20°C at night. Some sheltered places in the South such as Morro Jable may be a little warmer at night, but there isn't as pronounced a difference between localities as during winter and spring.

Rain?
Fuerteventura Airport receives a median of zero rainy days in June! Even if it does rain, it is unlikely to be over 0.1mm. In recent years (long term stats unavailable), Morro Jable in the South has received more rain than the northern part of the island at this time of year (the south is drier during the rest of the year). It's still nothing to worry about though, with less than half a millimetre over one or two days.

Cloud Cover

At the airport, there is usually only one overcast day during the entire month of June. However, other parts of the island may be cloudier. The Panza de burro cloud conditions can be predominant at this time of year – especially in the Western Canary Islands. These clouds affect the northern slopes of the islands, and in Fuerteventura, these clouds affect places such as Cofete, Corralejo or El Cotillo. This is especially so during the mornings, with the clouds often evaporating or 'burning' off by lunchtime.

Windy?
The summer trade winds will usually have taken hold by June providing a constant North-easterly breeze. While not the windiest month (July and August are windier), you may want to find beaches that have some protection to the north-east if the wind bothers you. Also, be aware that the cooling breeze can prevent you from realizing that you are being burned by the sun!

Calima
The Canary Islands are occasionally affected by easterly winds bringing dust from the Sahara. Although this phenomenon is more common during the winter months, if it does happen in June, the temperatures can soar (high 30s Celsius).

Sea Temperature
The sea is starting to warm up again in the Canary Islands in June, but is still a refreshing 21°C and a few degrees colder than the peak in late September.

July Weather in Fuerteventura

Daytime Highs

It will come as little surprise to most people that July is one of the warmest months of the year in Fuerteventura. Daily highs along the coast are in the upper 20s, with a long-term average daily high temperature of 27°C at the airport. Fortunately, the island is mostly spared the extreme high temperatures that places such as Andalusia in mainland Spain experience at this time of year. Coastal towns get an average of just 4 days with temperatures over 30°C, and 40°C is rare along the coast. Away from the sea, temperatures can be higher, and the all-time record high temperature for Fuerteventura was recorded in La Oliva in July 1994.

Nighttime Lows

Temperatures at night drop to about 20 – 22°C in July, with a few warmer nights. This is the perfect temperature to sit outside at night in summer clothes, though you may want air-conditioning in your room if you are not used to the heat.

Rain

In a word: unlikely. On average, there is some light rain on one day during July once every 5 years or so.

Cloud

July is the least cloudy month of the year on the island. There may be some days with thin cloud (that you'll still burn under), and the north of the island may get some cloudy mornings, but it will be mostly sunny with some haze.

Wind

The trade winds are at their strongest in the Canary Islands at this time of year, and July is the windiest month. For this reason, it is a very popular time of year with Wind and Kite Surfers who can be seen in action at windy spots such as the Sotavento Lagoon. If you don't like the wind, you can always seek out beaches that are sheltered from the North-east wind.

Sea Temperature
The sea temperature usually reaches 21 or 22°C at this time of year – and a little warmer in shallow water by the afternoon.

Calima
Although not very common at this time of year, if the wind does change to an easterly direction, then it can get very hot, with dust clouds blown across from the Sahara. This phenomenon is known in the Canaries as Calima (dust in Spanish).

August Weather in Fuerteventura

Daytime Highs
August is the hottest month of the year in Fuerteventura with daily highs of between about 27°C and 34°C at the Airport (East Coast). Other parts of the island, especially the interior and south, can be even hotter, reaching the high 30s or even 40s (Celsius).

Nighttime Lows
At night, temperatures don't usually drop below 20°C, with an average low of 21.5°C. In other words, the perfect

temperature to enjoy Tapas outside on a terrace at night, but air conditioning will be welcome back at your Hotel room.

Rain?
Rain is highly unusual in August, though in some years there may be a few brief drops should the weather come from the south. Rain above 0.1mm would be a freakish event at this time of year.

Cloud Cover
August is the sunniest month in Fuerteventura, though there may be some cloud cover in the morning in the north of the island. There is usually some haze even when the wind is from the north.

Wind
The Trade Winds tend to dominate at this time of year, and August has the second highest average wind speed (after July). That said, it doesn't tend to be gusty, just a constant breeze. It is often worth seeking out sheltered beaches, as some beaches (e.g. Playa Esmeralda) can be very windy at this time of year. It is also worth noting that the cooling effects of the wind mean that you might not realise that you are being sunburnt – the UV Index is pretty extreme in August in Fuerteventura.

Sea Temperature
The sea temperature is usually 22°C at this time of year and warmer at sheltered beaches and lagoons by the afternoon.

Calima (Dust from the Sahara)
If there is a Calima in August, it will be uncomfortably hot with temperatures of around 40°C. The air quality will be

pretty poor as well, and the local authorities may advise people not to exercise outdoors if it is a bad one.

September Weather in Fuerteventura

Daily High Temperatures
September is the second hottest month of the year in Fuerteventura (after August) with daytime highs of between 27 and 32°C. As always, temperatures may be a little higher in the south and interior of the island, as well as on terraces sheltered from the wind.

Nightly Low Temperatures
It will generally be quite warm at night, with lows of about 22°C. Great for sitting out in restaurant terraces at night, but you'll be glad to have air-conditioning in your hotel room.

Rain?
In most years, it doesn't rain at all in September with a median total precipitation of just 0.4mm. However, nothing is guaranteed, and in September 2022, there was a whopping 65.9mm of rain! A local newspaper reported that some parts of Fuerteventura received more rain in 24 hours than they had received during the previous 10 years combined.

Cloudy?
In September, it is mostly wall-to-wall sunshine, with perhaps a few cloudy mornings in the north of the island. You could, of course, be extremely unlucky and get freak rain, but September is generally regarded as one of the best times of year to visit the island.

Wind

By the end of the month, the Trade Winds begin to lose their dominance over the weather in Fuerteventura, making September less windy than July and August. There is usually still a breeze though, with the possibility of some still days – especially in the second half of the month.

Sea Temperature

The sea is at its warmest around Fuerteventura in September with a peak of between 22 and 24°C. As you might expect, the water will be even warmer in sheltered lagoons and in the shallows by late afternoon.

October Weather in Fuerteventura

With milder daytime temperatures, warm nights, a warm sea, little wind and mostly clear skies, October is considered by many to be the best time to visit Fuerteventura.

Daytime High Temperatures

Daily highs in October range from about 25 to 30°C with a median daytime high at Fuerteventura Airport of 25.9°C. There isn't much high temperature difference between the island's main resorts at this time of year. Temperatures may be a bit higher in the interior – especially on windless days.

Nightly Lows

At night, temperatures drop to around 20°C – perfect for al fresco dining. Anecdotal evidence suggests that the evenings in Costa Calma can be a bit cooler than other tourist resorts, so it might be a good idea to pack a light jacket or cardigan if you are staying there.

Rain

The first rains after the (normally) dry summer tend to arrive during the second half of the month – if they arrive at all. On average, there are 2 – 3 days with rain over 0.1mm, with an average total of 7.7mm. These numbers can be slightly misleading, and it's more likely that there will either be some torrential rain, a few drops or no rain at all.

Cloud

As usual, the northern half of the island can be a bit cloudier than the South – especially in the mornings. But it will mostly be lots of Sunshine!

Wind

October is the least windy month of the year in Fuerteventura with a median wind speed of 18kmph. Even some of the beaches favoured by windsurfers can be quite still at this time of year.

Sea Surface Temperatures

The sea remains around its yearly high temperature during the first half of the month at 22-24°C, before starting to drop slightly towards the end of the month. We also start to see the first Atlantic swells at this time of year, so some precaution should be used – especially on the North and West coasts.

November Weather in Fuerteventura

November is usually when the weather changes from the summer-like conditions that the island enjoys right up to the end of October, to the winter pattern with colder evenings and the occasional few days of rain. There seems to be quite a noticeable difference between the North and South of Fuerteventura at this time of year, with Morro Jable still feeling quite summery with mild nights, while the north may be a couple of degrees cooler. Expect a noticeable and sometimes quite abrupt change in the weather at some stage in November.

Daytime Highs

Average daily high temperatures are around 24°C in the North of the island, and about 25-26°C in the South. There are usually some days with highs in the high 20s or even low 30s (Celsius).

Nighttime Lows

The longer-term average nighttime low is 17.7°C, however in recent years, it has been warmer at night in November. In Morro Jable, many nights in November are now over 20°C, and in the North and East of the island, the minimum temperatures have been over 18°C. As previously stated, there can be an abrupt change to the weather at this time of year, and 16°C nights are possible, so a cardigan or light jacket is worth packing.

Rain

There is the chance of rain in November, with an average of 3-4 days with rain over 0.1mm during the month.

Clouds

The north of island can be quite cloudy at this time of year – especially in the morning, the far south tends to be sunnier. On average, the airport gets about 3 overcast days during November – making it the second most overcast month of the year (after December).

Wind
The trade winds aren't as constant at this time of year and November is one of the least windy months of the year on the island. The average wind speed at the airport is 18kmph.

Sea Temperature
The sea is still relatively warm in November around Fuerteventura, with an average of between 21 and 22°C.

December Weather in Fuerteventura

The weather can be quite mixed in Fuerteventura in December – there is a chance of several days of rain, but there could also be plenty of sunshine with mild evenings.

Daytime High Temperatures
Daily high temperatures range between 20 and 24°C, and don't usually ever go above 30°C at this time of year.

Nightly Lows
The average nighttime low is 15.9°C at Fuerteventura Airport in December, however this has trended warmer in recent years, and there may even be some 20°C nights (especially in the South of the island). Away from the sea, temperatures may be a couple of degrees cooler. Nighttime temperatures can vary a lot during December and are very hard to predict: it could be 13°C or it could be 21°C! Our advice is to bring bring a jacket and some warmer clothes for the evening.

Rain
December is, on average, the rainiest month of the year in Fuerteventura with 5 to 6 days of rain over 0.1mm.

Fuerteventura is a desert island though, and in some years there is no rain at all.

Cloud Cover
December can be one of the cloudier months in Fuerteventura with an average of around 3 completely overcast days during the month (at the Airport). As usual, the North of the island is cloudier than the south.

Wind
December is one of the least windy months on the island with an average wind speed of about 19kmph. While there can be some wet and windy days, there can also be some perfectly still sunny days.

Calima (Dust from the Sahara)
The Canary Islands can be affected by dust from the Sahara at this time of year if the wind turns to the east. However, since the Sahara is cooler in December, it does not bring soaring temperatures, just some unpleasant dusty haze.

Sea Temperatures
Sea Surface Temperatures drop to about 20°C at this time of year – on the cool side, but still okay for a quick refreshing dip on a sunny day. A summer wetsuit is advised if you plan to spend a long time in the water.

Sunset and Sunrise in December
The sun rises at around 07:45 and sets at around 18:00 in December.

9. Notes from the author

Fuerteventura is my favorite Island in the Canaries, since there's no other Island in the archipelago that can match it's beautiful beaches.
Fuerteventura has something to offer for all ages, and all tastes.

- Bird watching in La Parad.
- Hiking in 103 hiking trails.
- Landscape Photography on the Jandia Peninsula.
- Kite flying in Corralejo.

The list is endless, Fuerteventura will not disappoint, you will want to come back time and time again.
You may just want to spend your time relaxing, or want to buy a second home are even a home to retire, close to the beach or even up in the mountains. I first visited the Island in the late 1980's fell in love with the place and moved here in the late 1990's before buying my first villa on the golf course in Caleta.
I can honestly say, buying a home and living in Fuerteventura was the best time of my life.

References

"Valores climatológicos normales. Fuerteventura Aeropuerto"

Climate chart

Mancomunidades de la provincia de Palmas, Las (Canarias). Archived

population chart

NOTES

NOTES

NOTES

NOTES

NOTES

NOTES

NOTES

NOTES

NOTES

NOTES

Printed in Great Britain
by Amazon

26012091R00064